THE MUSICIAN SAYS

Also available in the
Words of Wisdom series:

The Architect Says
Laura S. Dushkes

The Chef Says
Nach Waxman and Matt Sartwell

The Designer Says
Sara Bader

The Filmmaker Says
Jamie Thompson Stern

The Inventor Says
Kevin Lippert

the
MUSICIAN
says

Quotes, Quips, and Words of Wisdom

compiled & edited by Benedetta LoBalbo

Princeton Architectural Press, New York

One of my earliest memories of music is of listening to a yellow 45 rpm record with a version of the Walt Whippo and Bernard Zaritzky song "The Little White Duck." It is a sweet song about a little white duck sittin' in the water, then a little green frog swimmin' in the water, then a little black bug floatin' on the water. All is well. Everyone is "doin' what [they] oughter" and happy to be who and what they are. The verses for the duck, the frog, and the little black bug are in a nice, light, bouncy major key. But when the little red snake is about to appear, the music turns to a minor key. At two years old, I didn't have words to explain it, but I remember that the change from major to minor frightened me. I knew something was going south at the pond. That half-step increment had the power to send my little legs running from the room. Just a chord change from major to minor was all it took.

Laura Nyro called music a "link with the divine." It is also a link with our humanity. Music can uplift us into laughter, or it can pull tears from us that we have long suppressed. The rising diminished chords in a suspenseful movie can set our hair on end. An unexpected or out-of-place note can make us laugh as hard as any play on words. And when the combined forces of music and lyrics touch us, they can be transcendent.

Researching this book has been an extensive, exciting romp through the world of musicians: singers, songwriters, instrumentalists, composers, film scorers—anyone who has a relationship with the Muse and has experienced the sacrifices, joys, and frustrations it brings. As a singer/songwriter, I understand the dance with the Muse that can leave one exhilarated in one moment and downtrodden in the next. If you are a musician, I hope you will experience a sense of belonging and gratitude for the privilege of being one who has the gift of expressing thoughts and feelings that lie beyond everyday language.

In this collection, you'll hear from an eclectic group of much-loved musicians, spanning the globe and the centuries. Brian Eno and Leonard Bernstein reflect on their earliest musical influences; Vladimir Horowitz and Billy Joel reveal those final moments before they walk out on stage; John Lennon and Beethoven talk about how inspiration visited them unannounced in the middle of the night; Björk and Neko Case emphasize the experience and excitement of live shows; and Mozart and Tommy Ramone discuss the fine art of keeping time. With one quote per page, each spread becomes its own exchange between two talents creating their own riffs about the blessings and curses of being a musician.

The process of compiling and editing their thoughts was much like scoring a piece of music. There were recurring themes that I wanted to carry through. They needed to segue into the next topic, or perhaps the timing called for a complete departure—time to introduce a new motif. There were the legato passages—the long quotes—and the staccato exchanges—the short, punchy one-sentence messages. The themes that carried through needed to crescendo at the right moment. A quote that relayed the same message as another was chosen because of wording that was much funnier or more poignant, or because it provided a counterpoint to a different quote. Sometimes pure inspiration would illuminate a pairing that I hadn't considered. And through this all, my editor played the role of producer, choosing the best vehicle and the optimal moment, seeing the big picture and total arrangement.

As I worked on this book, I was introduced to artists I hadn't known before. I loved the opportunity to discover their work and listen to their music for the first time. I hope these pages offer you the same adventure.

PS: The little red snake ate the little black bug. No ducks or frogs were harmed in the making of the record.

Music is indeed the most beautiful of all Heaven's gifts to humanity wandering in the darkness. Alone it calms, enlightens, and stills our souls.

Pyotr Ilyich Tchaikovsky (1840-93)

THERE IS OLD ENERGY THAT COMES FROM SOMEWHERE AND PASSES THROUGH US. CREATING MUSIC IS USING THIS ENERGY TO COMMUNICATE WITH AN AUDIENCE, LIKE BEING A MESSENGER.

Kitaro (1953-)

Music circulates because of the vibration, and so you have to be very careful what you put out.

Yoko Ono (1933-)

I can't think of anything else that's as close to magic. I'm totally useless in the real world.... My whole life takes place in some sort of imaginary place, and I worked bloody hard to never have to grow up.

Hans Zimmer (1957–)

When I was a child, I told my parents that I wanted to be a musician when I grew up, and they told me I had to pick one or the other.

Ledward Kaapana (1948–)

The first song I wrote was a song to Brigitte Bardot.

Bob Dylan (1941-)

One of my earliest musical memories is **a song called "Boa Constrictor"**—sung by Johnny Cash and written by the brilliant Shel Silverstein. The recording ends with the boa constrictor belching— which to a five-year-old is, of course, the pinnacle of cerebral humor.

"Weird Al" Yankovic (1959–)

I think the first time I knew what
I wanted to do with my life was
when I was about four years old.
I was listening to an old Victrola,
playing a railroad song. The
song was called "Hobo Bill's Last
Ride." And I thought that was the
most wonderful, amazing thing
that I'd ever seen. That you could
take this piece of wax, and music
would come out of that box.
From that day on, I wanted to
sing on the radio.

Johnny Cash (1932-2003)

The Grand Ole Opry used to come on, and I used to watch that. They used to have some pretty heavy cats, heavy guitar players.

Jimi Hendrix (1942–70)

I can remember at an early point in my life hearing doo-wop for the first time.... It could have been from another galaxy, for all I knew. I was absolutely entranced by it, from the age of seven or eight.... I had never heard music like this, and one of the reasons it was beautiful was because it came without a context.... Now, in later life, I realized that this removal of context was an important point in the magic of music.

Brian Eno (1948–)

When I was ten, an aunt of mine in Boston decided to move to New York. She dumped some of her heavier furniture at our house, and in the load was a piano.... And that was it. That was my contract with life, with God. From then on, that's what I knew I had to do. I had found my universe, my place where I felt safe.

Leonard Bernstein (1918-90)

I played all classical music when I was in the orphanage. That instills the soul in you. You know? Liszt, Bach, Rachmaninoff, Gustav Mahler, and Haydn.

Louis Armstrong (1901–71)

The tree grows up and branches out, but it is the roots that give it substance. So roots is very important to keep in music. If you lose the root, the tree dies.

Ziggy Marley (1968–)

I TAUGHT MYSELF FROM ABOUT THE AGE OF FIFTEEN. I LEARNED A FEW CHORDS WHEN I WAS YOUNGER AND JUST LISTENED TO MUSIC AND TRIED TO REPLICATE IT, BLUES FIRST AND THEN A LONG CLUMSY PROCESS OF JUST LEARNING SONGS I LOVED.

Hozier (1990–)

I never took lessons. I once thought I was losing my voice years ago, and I hired a teacher.... He said, "Well you know, I teach the Streisand method." I said, "What IS the Streisand method?" I had no idea what he was talking about.

Barbra Streisand (1942–)

I remember when I was
in fourth grade we had
talent shows, and I played
"Baby Elephant Walk,"
a Henry Mancini tune,
and when I couldn't figure
out the rest of the piece
I made it up.

Diana Krall (1964-)

Music had just been a tool of torture and control in my life up until I was twelve. I was watching *The Ed Sullivan Show*, and when I saw The Beatles, music became something that was really great. I practiced Beatles songs, and **for a long time I fantasized that I was the fifth Beatle.** When each one needed to take a break while onstage, they would just nod at me, and I would jump up and fill in without missing a beat.

Mark Mothersbaugh (1950-)

LISTENING TO THE BEATLES HAD A HUGE INFLUENCE ON ME.

Rosanne Cash (1955-)

For me, music has always been additive, never subtractive. If I fall in love with something, I always love it. So for me, The Beatles are still in the house.

Vernon Reid (1958–)

EVERYONE STEALS FROM EVERYONE ELSE.

Bruce Springsteen (1949-)

So sing, change.
Add to. Subtract. But
beware multiplying.
If you record and start
making hundreds
of copies, watch out.
Write a letter first.
Get permission.

Pete Seeger (1919–2014)

Don't mutilate your foot, trying to squeeze it into Cinderella's slipper.

Joe Jackson (1954–)

If you're doing your job right, you're not going to be like anybody else, and you're going to get the opportunities that other people don't get and vice versa. And you'll drive yourself crazy comparing too much.

Dar Williams (1967–)

My relationship with my muse is a delicate one at the best of times, and I feel that it is my duty to protect her from influences that may offend her fragile nature.... My muse is not a horse and I am in no horse race.

Nick Cave (1957–)

[I] always long for that time and that space…that block of time where I can go on a writing binge. Because I'm addicted to my songwriting.

Dolly Parton (1946–)

MUSIC BREEDS ITS OWN INSPIRATION. YOU CAN ONLY DO IT BY DOING IT. YOU JUST SIT DOWN AND YOU MAY NOT FEEL LIKE IT, BUT YOU PUSH YOURSELF. IT'S A WORK PROCESS.

Burt Bacharach (1928-)

I just write when I feel like it. Day or night, no matter where I am, that takes precedent. That's the only rule I have.

Neil Young (1945–)

Songwriting is a very strange thing. . . . It's not something that I can say, "Next Tuesday morning, I'm gonna sit down and write songs." I can't do that. No way. If I say, "I'm going to the country and take a walk in the woods next Tuesday," then the probability is, next Tuesday night I might write a song.

Johnny Cash (1932–2003)

I still think you have to wait for the inspiration, but unless you're there, waiting at the bus stop, you ain't gonna get on the bus.

David Byrne (1952–)

IF I KNEW WHERE THE GOOD SONGS CAME FROM, I'D GO THERE MORE OFTEN. IT'S A MYSTERIOUS CONDITION. IT'S MUCH LIKE THE LIFE OF A CATHOLIC NUN. YOU'RE MARRIED TO A MYSTERY.

Leonard Cohen (1934-)

THE SECRET OF A GREAT MELODY IS A SECRET.

Dave Brubeck (1920–2012)

It seems like there's a board there, and all the nails are pounded in all over the place,... and every new person that comes to pound in a nail finds that there's one less space.... I'm content with the same old piece of wood. I just want to find another place to pound in a nail.

Bob Dylan (1941–)

With most of the songs I've ever written, quite honestly, I've felt there's an enormous gap here, waiting to be filled; this song should have been written hundreds of years ago. How did nobody pick up on that little space?... And you say, I don't believe they've missed that fucking hole!

Keith Richards (1943-)

I always have a notebook...
with me, and when an idea
comes to me, I put it down
at once. I even get up in the
middle of the night when
a thought comes, because
otherwise I might forget it.

Ludwig van Beethoven (1770–1827)

It's like being possessed…. It won't let you sleep, so you have to get up, make it into something, and then you're allowed to sleep. That's always in the middle of the bloody night, when you're half awake or tired and your critical facilities are switched off.

John Lennon (1940–80)

As I was on the street and these ideas would come, I would run into the corner store, the bodega, and grab, like, a paper bag.... And then I'd write the words on the paper bag and stuff these ideas in my pocket till I got back. And then I would transfer them into the notebook. And as I got further and further away [from] home and from the notebook, I had to memorize these rhymes longer and longer and longer— and, like with any exercise,... once you train your brain to do that, it becomes a natural occurrence.

Jay Z (1969-)

BEFORE TAPE RECORDERS I JUST HAD TO KEEP IT ALL IN MY HEAD.

John Lee Hooker (1917–2001)

YOU'VE GOT TO IGNORE THE FACTS TO TELL THE TRUTH.

Ani DiFranco (1970–)

It's very helpful to start with something that's true. If you start with something that's false, you're always covering your tracks.

Paul Simon (1941-)

Some things I can't talk about, but I can write about and pretend it's a third person. And that way I get it off my chest, and I know what it means.

Tammy Wynette (1942-98)

Sometimes I don't even know what I'm writing about when I'm writing about it. I'm speaking to something I don't understand, until about five years later.

Jenny Lewis (1976-)

ALL THOSE SONGS YOU'VE WRITTEN HAVE PROBABLY GOT A COUPLE GOOD LINES IN 'EM. THROW OUT EVERYTHING BUT THOSE AND START OVER. THEN BUILD THOSE UP ON A COUPLE SONGS—THEN COMBINE THE TWO. THAT'S IT. **BE RUTHLESS.**

Warren Zevon (1947–2003)

Children make up the best songs. . . . Kids are always working on songs and then throwing them away, like little origami things or paper airplanes. They don't care if they lose it; they'll just make another one.

Tom Waits (1949–)

Don't let the critic become bigger than the creator.

Randy Newman (1943-)

DON'T BE AFRAID TO WRITE A BAD SONG, BECAUSE THE NEXT ONE MAY BE GREAT.

Gerry Goffin (1939-2014)

If I'm listening to my
music, it's always,
Why didn't I put a guitar
fill in there? Why did
I read that line like that?
Why am I whining?

Joni Mitchell (1943–)

By the time I finish working on an album, I never want to hear it again in my life.

Frank Zappa (1940–93)

The lyric must never let go of the listener for a single instant. It's like fishing. A little slack in the line and they're off the hook.

Oscar Hammerstein II (1895-1960)

Because music has such a direct emotional force... you're able often to give enormous color and depth to something if you play a subtext in the orchestra that belies or undercuts the lyrics and vice versa. It keeps songs alive.

Stephen Sondheim (1930-)

I don't think you can compare rock as a work of art to a painting by Raphael or a great poem by Keats or Baudelaire. Yet rock does have a great visceral power. That's the power of music: it's very emotional.

Mick Jagger (1943-)

That's a very, very sad song. Extremely sad. Then I put a cello on it, for God's sake. What was I trying to do, kill people?

Dan Fogelberg (1951–2007)

MY MAIN INSTRUMENT
IS DRUMS, SO WHERE I HAVE
PURE MUSICAL FREEDOM
IS ON THEM, WHEREAS
ON GUITAR AND PIANO I HAVE
SOME LIMITATIONS. I FEEL,
HARMONICALLY SPEAKING,
I PAINT PRIMARY COLORS.

Hawksley Workman (1975-)

I don't play guitar or piano very well, but it seems to me as though it's easier to write on instruments I can't play too well.

Steven Tyler (1948-)

BO, WHICH I STILL HAVE AND TREASURE, BECAME MY TRUE GUITAR. ON IT, I HAVE WRITTEN THE GREATER MEASURE OF MY SONGS.

Patti Smith (1946–)

I never thought I'd have a guitar like that. It's older than my dad, this piece of wood. And I do believe that guitars have souls.

Jake Bugg (1994–)

I can see every minute of John and I writing together, playing together, recording together. I still have very vivid memories of all of that. It's not like it fades.

Paul McCartney (1942–)

What happened between Oscar [Hammerstein II] and me was almost chemical. Put the right components together and an explosion takes place.

Richard Rodgers (1902-79)

YOU HAVE TO SURROUND YOURSELF WITH MUSICIANS WHO THINK, NOT ONES WHO ARE COMFORTABLE.

Miles Davis (1926–91)

When I play, what
I try to do is to reach
my subconscious
level. I don't want to
overtly think about
anything, because you
can't think and play
at the same time—
believe me, I've tried it.
It goes by too fast.

Sonny Rollins (1930-)

I have never practiced more than an hour a day in my life.

Luciano Pavarotti (1935–2007)

I'm a perfectionist, and one thing about me: I practice until my feet bleed.

Beyoncé Knowles (1981–)

Good singing is a form of good acting.

Judy Garland (1922-69)

ALL SINGERS ARE METHOD ACTING.... THE ART OF ART IS TO BE AS REAL AS YOU CAN WITHIN THIS ARTIFICIAL SITUATION.

Joni Mitchell (1943-)

You could probably do a psychological study on trumpet players. I don't know if it's a need to be the center of attention, but I think we need to be heard. The trumpet is not one of those instruments that you can hide behind. You hit a couple of clams on the horn when you're playing in a section or a small group—it's really heard.

Herb Alpert (1935-)

I tend to think of cellists as nice people. There's less of a demand for us than for violinists or pianists. We're not sought after, so the image is different. Most of us have played in orchestras; we play a lot of chamber music; we have to work with other people all the time.

Yo-Yo Ma (1955–)

EVERYONE IS AMAZED THAT I CAN ALWAYS KEEP STRICT TIME.

Wolfgang Amadeus Mozart (1756–91)

When we first started rehearsing, Dee Dee [Ramone] was the lead singer, and he would count off the songs, and we just thought it was the most hilarious thing we ever heard.... **His counts had absolutely nothing to do with the speed of the songs.** He would count off a song and when he said the word four, we would just come in at the right speed.

Tommy Ramone (1949–2014)

I found there were a certain number of chord progressions to play in a given time, and sometimes what I played didn't work out in eighth notes, sixteenth notes, or triplets. I had to put the notes in uneven groups like fives and sevens in order to get them all in.

John Coltrane (1926-67)

Everybody tried to simulate Charlie Parker. He was carrying the torch of changing the music. What it involved was lots of energy. The chord changes had changed.... It was faster, it was quicker, it was a risk-taking music.

Betty Carter (1929–98)

It's just music.... It's trying to play clean and looking for the pretty notes.

Charlie "Bird" Parker (1920–55)

When I hear somebody play a pretty melody and then improvise off that melody and play other pretty melodies, **that really knocks me out.**

Stanley Clarke (1951–)

I like B flat. And I like F.

Jimmy Webb (1946–)

THE ORIGINAL KEY IS USUALLY THE BEST.

Neil Young (1945–)

I try things and experiment. I get lost—a lot of people get lost—but the other guys in the group can tell if you're lost, and one of them will establish something to let you know where you are.

Herbie Hancock (1940-)

When I sit down at the piano, it's always a challenge with me. I'm always exploring. Every time I sit down, I'm looking for chord changes, new ideas. And sometimes I do get tied up in a knot. When you see me smiling up there, I'm lost, trying to find a way to get out.

Earl "Fatha" Hines (1903–83)

You make a mistake, and that happens to take you in a new direction. Without that mistake you stay in the same place.

Giovanni Hidalgo (1963-)

I'm no longer afraid
of making mistakes.
I make them
every night during
a performance....
Wherever my voice
goes, wherever it takes
me I just follow it.

Bobby McFerrin (1950-)

At each concert I will play some wrong notes. But if the performance is great, it doesn't matter.

Arthur Rubinstein (1887–1982)

I've always carried a tool box….You're down to your last guitar cord. Someone trips over it, shorts it. Soldering under fire is part of the manual.

Garth Hudson (1937-)

It's not that we've never written
a set list. At least once every tour
I try to write one, but we have
never in the history of this band—
and probably in the history of
all my bands—actually played the
set list that I wrote, so there's
always a lot of messing around....
A lot of improvising between tunes,
during tunes, in spite of tunes.

Marc Ribot (1954-)

When we hit the bandstand, everybody's coming from twenty different directions. I'm always amazed that we ever get a show done.... We never do sound checks, and we never rehearse. That way, it's bound to sound different every night.

Willie Nelson (1933–)

I still believe that you reap what you sow on tour. If you're touring, you're really planting personal seeds in the fans. I'm very one-on-one.

Katy Perry (1984–)

MY FIRST BIG GIGS WERE OPENING A SHOW FOR FRANK ZAPPA, AND I THINK THAT WAS DIFFICULT. I WAS KIND OF LIKE THE RECTAL THERMOMETER FOR THE AUDIENCE.

Tom Waits (1949–)

I try not to be nervous before a concert. Not to rush. All the movements quiet.

Vladimir Horowitz (1903–89)

I get asked, "Do you have a ritual? What do you do before you go on stage?" I walk from the dressing room to the stage, that's the ritual.

Billy Joel (1949–)

*I was received with such
enthusiasm that I went pale
and red; it did not cease even
when I had already seated
myself at the piano....
You can imagine that this
gave me courage since
I had been shaking all
over with anxiety. I played
as I can hardly ever
remember having played.*

Clara Schumann (1819-96)

There's nothing like an audience at the Apollo. They were wide awake early in the morning. They didn't ask me what my style was, who I was, how I had evolved, where I'd come from, who influenced me, or anything. They just broke the house up. And they kept right on doing it.

Billie Holiday (1915–59)

This is either where
you prove the people who
like you right, or prove
the people who hate you
right. It's up to you.
Put on your banjo and
go play.

Taylor Swift (1989-)

I WANT THEM TO WALK OUT OF THAT THEATER HAPPY. AND TO BE SAYING, "JESUS, HOW DOES THAT OLD BROAD DO IT?"

Lena Horne (1917–2010)

THE FACT THAT PEOPLE ARE FINDING SO MUCH STUFF ONLINE MEANS THEY NEED TO GO TO SHOWS MORE.... PEOPLE ARE ALWAYS GOING TO NEED PHYSICALITY.

Björk (1965-)

A live show is one of the last holdouts of a thing that makes you feel a part of a community, where you'll go and maybe meet your future wife or boyfriend, or you're taking your sister to her first show. These are the things that you remember later in your life.

Neko Case (1970–)

Going out to hear music is really important.

Esperanza Spalding (1984-)

I hate going to concerts because I hate parking my car.

Gordon Lightfoot (1938–)

Touring was exhausting. And that's another big surprise because it doesn't sound like it's going to be difficult; it sounds like it's going to be fun. And then you sort of start to understand those reports of "So-and-so was hospitalized for exhaustion."

Aimee Mann (1960-)

THE BIGNESS OF METALLICA—I'M KIND OF TIRED OF IT. YOU MIGHT LOOK AT IT AS A FRIEND. TO ME IT'S BEEN A BEAST, AND IT'S KIND OF SUCKED A LOT OF ME INTO IT.

James Hetfield (1963–)

Amid the noise and stink and chaos of the road, the van was our only sanctuary. Once we got out of the van, punk rock was all around us. So we kept the van very clean.... And while we drove from town to town, there was very little talking for hours on end. We barely even played music in the van. It was a time to recharge and rest.

Bob Mould (1960–)

It's manic. That's the best way I can describe it. You go from an arena of eighty thousand people to a tour bus where you're all alone, from a place where the decibel level is so loud you can almost see it to absolute silence.

Justin Timberlake (1981–)

I certainly could not marry.... For to me there is no greater pleasure than to practice and exercise my art.

Ludwig van Beethoven (1770–1827)

If there's anything fit to worship, I think it's music.

St. Vincent (1982–)

Musicians don't call it working; they call it playing. There's a reason. You haven't actually worked an honest day in your life.

Bruce Springsteen (1949-)

It certainly feels like manual labor some days, though I'm mighty glad I'm not on a building site mixing cement!

Billy Bragg (1957-)

I think the best thing to keep you in shape creatively is to keep yourself in shape physically. I run, I swim, I do whatever I can to try to keep myself together.

Mose Allison (1927–)

Depression doesn't take away your talents— it just makes them harder to find.

Lady Gaga (1986-)

There are two plottable curves— as the increase of drugs curve went up the amount of songs and creativity curve went down at the same rate.

David Crosby (1941-)

YOU DO WHAT YOU LOVE…OR YOU GET ARRESTED.

Lou Reed (1942–2013)

My concert took place at eleven o'clock this morning. It was a splendid success from the point of view of honor and glory, but a failure as far as money was concerned.

Wolfgang Amadeus Mozart (1756-91)

I'm wondering where the eight million dollars that I earned in the last ten years has gone.

Steven Tyler (1948-)

A rock star is someone with a hole in his heart almost the size of his ego.

Bono (1960–)

I'M NOT A DORK. I'M A FUCKING ROCK STAR.

Win Butler (1980-)

IF YOU ACT LIKE A ROCK STAR, YOU WILL BE TREATED LIKE ONE.

Marilyn Manson (1969-)

This might sound cocky, but I'm the only person out here doing what I'm doing. If I'm not cocky, people are just going to pass me by, and the record company will try to make me do things I don't want to do. You just have to be real strong.

Harry Connick Jr. (1967–)

There's a path you have to take to become a pop icon or a pop star and a really different path to become an R&B star.... And I really like just being me and trying to figure out who I am.

Meshell Ndegeocello (1968–)

I said I don't want to be a singles artist, and I don't want to change what I look like. I'm not that beautiful, and I don't want to be a pop star. I won't take any advance money, but just let me have complete control of when I put it out, who I'm gonna work with, and what the songs are. And I'll work my ass off.

Bonnie Raitt (1949-)

TRUST YOUR TALENT. YOU DON'T HAVE TO MAKE A WHORE OUT OF YOURSELF TO GET AHEAD. YOU REALLY DON'T.

Bette Midler (1945-)

You've got to be a bastard in this business.

David Bowie (1947-)

The name Blondie is an established trademark. It's a business thing.

Debbie Harry (1945–)

Everything has changed for me since I've changed my name. It's one thing to be called Prince but it's better to actually be one.

Prince (1958–)

I am Warhol.
I am the No. 1 most
impactful artist
of our generation.
I am Shakespeare
in the flesh.
Walt Disney.
Nike. Google.

Kanye West (1977–)

I'm happy to be out of the fray, doing whatever I want to do, considered by many, if not most, to be some eccentric has-been.

Pete Townshend (1945-)

Cher's great. She gets better as she gets older even though she keeps complaining that it sucks and saying how much she hates it…. She just comes on and does her thing.

Chrissie Hynde (1951-)

I'M NOT A HUGE CHER FAN.

Cher (1946-)

YOU KNOW YOU'RE ON TOP WHEN THEY START THROWING ARROWS AT YOU. EVEN JESUS WAS CRUCIFIED.

Michael Jackson (1958-2009)

Offstage, I started believing
I had to be Alice all the time…
till I realized, "What am
I doing this for? Bela Lugosi
doesn't go biting people in the
neck offstage."

Alice Cooper (1948–)

In order to win applause one must write stuff which is so inane that a coachman could sing it, or so unintelligible that it pleases precisely because no sensible man can understand it.

Wolfgang Amadeus Mozart (1756–91)

Ignore your lawyer and manager and anyone else who has an opinion when it comes to your songs. Go with your gut, write for yourself, and block out all that noise.

Suzanne Vega (1959–)

I think one of the things that's going to be nauseatingly characteristic about so much music of now is its glossy production values and its griddedness, the tightness of the way everything is locked together.

Brian Eno (1948–)

What is Auto-Tune? I don't even know what Auto-Tune is.

Aretha Franklin (1942–)

Most bands don't work out. A small-unit democracy is very, very difficult. Very, very difficult.

Bruce Springsteen (1949-)

The longer we're a band,
the more painfully
obvious it becomes why
most bands don't last.
It's probably the nature
of anything that starts
out small and self-directed,
and becomes larger and
in danger of not being
self-directed.

Richard Reed Parry (1977-)

For me the music community was always like a model for what could be. The way people would play together, just harmony and being—old guys and young guys, black guys and white guys. It was setting an example for what the rest of us could be.

Bill Frisell (1951-)

I didn't know Chuck Berry was black for two years after I first heard his music…. And for ages I didn't know Jerry Lee Lewis was white.

Keith Richards (1943-)

*I'd like to think that when
I sing a song, I can let you know
all about the heartbreak,
struggle, lies, and kicks in the
ass I've gotten over the years
for being black and everything
else, without actually saying
a word about it.*

Ray Charles (1930-2004)

To me music is such a personal thing; everything in your life is coming out in your music. You can't really eliminate social and political views from your music—it's in there.

Dexter Gordon (1923-90)

MY SONG IS MY LIFE.

Édith Piaf (1915–63)

LE CONCERT, C'EST MOI.

Franz Liszt (1811–86)

Some people liked me, hated me, walked with me, walked over me, jeered me, cheered me, rooted me and hooted me, and before long I was invited in and booted out of every public place of entertainment in that country. But I decided that songs was a music and a language of all tongues.

Woody Guthrie (1912–67)

Something I learned…
from Woody Guthrie:
he talks about how people
pay more attention if you
sing about topical issues.
I guess that was what
we were trying to do, in our
own way. We were trying
to encapsulate what
we were seeing around us
and put it into music.

Jay Farrar (1966-)

Rock and roll in the Sixties
and Seventies was shooting for
an idealism, a utopianism,
that is still worth shooting for.
It is exactly what sensible, logical,
pragmatic, well-rounded,
disciplined Western civilization
needs. We need to open our
hearts a bit, which was
something we had time for
in the Sixties.

Pete Townshend (1945-)

ROCK AND ROLL, AT ITS CORE, IS MERELY A BUNCH OF RAVING SHIT.

Lester Bangs (1948–82)

The blues come from way back. When the world was born, the blues was born. As the world progressed, the blues got more fancy and more modern. They dressed it up much more. They got lyrics now that they didn't have then. But they're still saying the same thing.

John Lee Hooker (1917–2001)

I WAS ATTRACTED TO THE SOUND AND THE CONTENT AND THE FREEDOM OF RAP. TO ME, IT'S LIKE A FREE ART FORM. IT FLOWS. IT'S SMOOTH. IT CAN BE ANYTHING YOU WANT IT TO BE.

Queen Latifah (1970-)

Words symbolize the body, and jubilant music reveals the spirit.

Hildegard von Bingen (1098-1179)

I AIM TO HIT PEOPLE IN THE CHEST WITH MY GROOVE AND HIT THEM IN THE HEART WITH MY MELODIES. I DON'T CARE AS MUCH ABOUT HITTING THEM IN THE BRAIN.

Damian Erskine (1973-)

They say even
iron wears out. I
think if I ever just
had to sit down,
I'd say to myself,
"What am I going
to do now?"

Ella Fitzgerald (1917–96)

I think I will get
the message when
it's time for me
to stop. I'm sure
somebody will say,
"Okay, Diana Ross,
it's enough now."

Diana Ross (1944–)

We're fighting people's misconceptions about what rock and roll is supposed to be. You're supposed to do it when you're twenty, twenty-five— as if you're a tennis player and you have three hip surgeries and you're done. We play rock and roll because it's what turned us on. Muddy Waters and Howlin' Wolf—the idea of retiring was ludicrous to them. You keep going—and why not?

Keith Richards (1943-)

Well, Keith, now Keith, he can play forever because he's looked like he was about a hundred and fifty since he was twenty-five, and he's rhythm and blues, so he can keep going forever.... But there's a time to give it up.

Grace Slick (1939-)

I hope that what
I leave behind
will grow through
someone else and
become better
than where I was
able to take it.

Stevie Wonder (1950-)

There are so many people to thank, but I hear the wrap-up music starting, so I'll make this quick. I'll begin with the person who managed the astonishing nuts and bolts of putting a book like this together. Sara Stemen, my editor at Princeton Architectural Press, deserves a standing ovation for her masterful insights into the tempo and dynamics of this collection. My appreciation to PAPress for giving me the opportunity to explore, enjoy, and elucidate what the musician says—I'm proud to be a part of this series. Special thanks to Paul Wagner, the design director; Jan Haux, for the artful presentation of the musicians' words; and Janet Behning, who diligently oversaw, with keen attention to detail, the production process.

Thanks to all the musicians—those included within these pages and those out in the world sharing their sounds—especially to John, Paul, George, and Ringo, who rocked my world. My deepest gratitude to Sara Bader, who thought of me for this project, for her encouragement and faith in me. I am indebted to my father and mother, Charles and Marian, for placing me on that piano stool at five years old, and to Anthony, Teresa, and Kyle.

Published by
Princeton Architectural Press
A McEvoy Group company
202 Warren Street
Hudson, New York 12534

Visit our website at www.papress.com

Developmental editor: Sara Bader
Project editor: Sara Stemen
Designer: Jan Haux
Series designer: Paul Wagner

Special thanks to: Nicola Bednarek Brower, Janet Behning, Erin Cain,
Megan Carey, Carina Cha, Andrea Chlad, Tom Cho, Barbara Darko,
Benjamin English, Jan Cigliano Hartman, Mia Johnson, Diane Levinson,
Jennifer Lippert, Jaime Nelson, Rob Shaeffer, Marielle Suba,
Kaymar Thomas, Joseph Weston, and Janet Wong of
Princeton Architectural Press —Kevin C. Lippert, publisher

Library of Congress Cataloging-in-Publication Data
The musician says : quotes, quips, and words of wisdom / compiled &
edited by Benedetta LoBalbo.—First edition.
159 pages ; 19 cm — (Words of wisdom)
Includes index.
ISBN 978-1-61689-389-7 (alk. paper)
1. Music—Quotations, maxims, etc. 2. Musicians—Quotations, maxims,
etc. I. LoBalbo, Benedetta, compiler.
PN6084.M8.M88 2015
780—dc23
                                                    2014046793

I guess I'd like
people to say
I played in tune,
that I played in
good taste, and
that I was nice
to people.
That's about it.

Chet Atkins (1924–2001)